ARMORED DINOSAURS

AND THEIR SCARY SPIKES, SPINES, AND HORNS!

PAUL HARRISON

ARCTURUS

WHAT IS A DINOSAUR?

The word "dinosaur" means "terrible lizard," although a dinosaur is not a lizard but a type of reptile. There were hundreds of different types of dinosaur and they were real record breakers—the biggest, heaviest, longest, tallest creatures ever to have walked the planet. The first dinosaur remains were found in Connecticut in the early 19th century, followed by more discoveries in southern England. Since then, dinosaur fossils have been discovered all over the world.

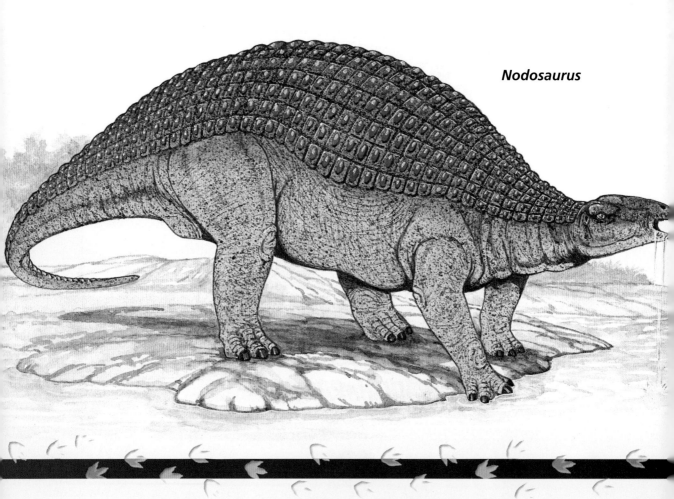

Nodosaurus

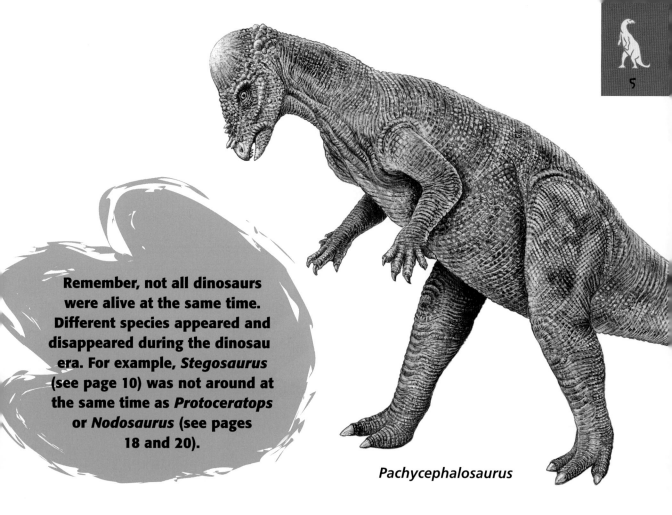

Remember, not all dinosaurs were alive at the same time. Different species appeared and disappeared during the dinosau era. For example, *Stegosaurus* (see page 10) was not around at the same time as *Protoceratops* or *Nodosaurus* (see pages 18 and 20).

Pachycephalosaurus

Dinosaurs are a large yet very specific group of creatures. To qualify, an animal has to satisfy a number of criteria:

1 It must have lived during the Mesozoic era, which is divided into three periods, called the Triassic, Jurassic, and Cretaceous. The Triassic lasted from 245 million years ago (mya) to 208 mya, the Jurassic from 208 mya to 145 mya, and the Cretaceous from 145 mya to the end of the dinosaurs (65 mya).

2 It must be a reptile, although not all reptiles are dinosaurs. For example, lizards are reptiles, but they are not dinosaurs.

3 Its legs must be located below its body, giving it an erect stance, as opposed to sticking out from the sides, like those of a crocodile.

4 It must have lived on land, not in the air like pterosaurs, or in the water like swimming reptiles.

TRICERATOPS

One of the most famous dinosaurs ever, this big bruiser of a plant-eater was one of the most common Cretaceous dinosaurs.

Pointy

Triceratops is famous for the three sharp horns on its head, which give it its name. Partly for display but mainly for defense, these three prongs were equally as effective in scaring off carnivores (and rival males) as they were in attracting females. The formidable horns, particularly the pair of 3-foot-long upper horns, were more than sharp enough to kill anything in their way—which was why all but the biggest or smartest carnivores were tempted to give *Triceratops* a wide berth.

TRIASSIC · JURASSIC · CRETACEOUS

Fact File

How to say it tri-SER-ra-tops
Meaning of name Three-horned face
Family Ceratopidae
Period Late Cretaceous
Where found USA
Height 10 feet (3 meters)
Length 30 feet (9 meters)
Weight 6 tons (5,400 kilograms)
Food Plants
Special features Horns and frill

Frilly

Of course, the horns were only effective if *Triceratops* was facing its foe. What happened if it was attacked from behind? If a meat-eater tried to grab *Triceratops* around the neck, as lions do to their prey, then its huge, bony crest should have stopped its attacker achieving a clean bite—long enough, with any luck, for *Triceratops* to shake it off.

Paleontologists think *Triceratops* formed a circle when under attack, facing outward. Spiky!

ANKYLOSAURUS

This was the last and possibly the most famous of the ankylosaurids. *Ankylosaurus* was big, wide, heavy, and covered in bony plates. Most predators would have thought twice before tackling this well-protected dinosaur.

Bulky

Ankylosaurus's body was all about defense; it was covered in thick plates of bone fused into the dinosaur's skin. This formed a hard, shell-like structure over the creature; it even had bony plates over its eyes. Its body was also covered in rows of short spikes, and for good measure it had a heavy, bony club at the end of its tail.

Under attack

If *Ankylosaurus* found itself cornered in an attack, rather than run it would crouch low to the ground to protect its underbelly. This meant the predator had to try to flip it over to get at the soft part underneath. However, this was difficult for two reasons: first, *Ankylosaurus* was very, very heavy, and second, the spikes on its body made it even harder to overturn. Plus, there was always a danger of getting clubbed by that dangerous tail. It could easily break a predator's leg, and a badly injured dinosaur was likely to end up as lunch itself for another meat-eater—one more good reason for predators to find easier prey.

Fact File

How to say it ang-KEY-loh-SORE-us
Meaning of name Stiff lizard
Family Ankylosauridae
Period Late Cretaceous
Where found Canada, USA
Height 4 feet (1.2 meters)
Length 23 feet (7 meters)
Weight 4.4 tons (4,000 kilograms)
Food Plants
Special features Heavily armored body

Food

Squat, heavy *Ankylosaurus* had little choice but to eat low-growing plants. Fortunately, this creature was not a fussy eater, as its wide mouth demonstrates, and it was happy munching on any plant that it stumbled across.

Ankylosaurus had a very small brain in relation to its body size—but then it didn't really need to think much!

TRIASSIC   JURASSIC   CRETACEOUS

STEGOSAURUS

Stegosaurus was the largest member of the stegosaur family—a wide-ranging group of large plant-eating dinosaurs found around the world.

Pointless plates?

The most impressive features of *Stegosaurus* were undoubtedly the two rows of plates running down its back. When these were first observed, paleontologists presumed they were for defense; we now know this wasn't the case. Firstly, the plates were too weak to hold off another dinosaur. Secondly, they wouldn't really protect the most vulnerable parts of the dinosaur, such as its belly region.

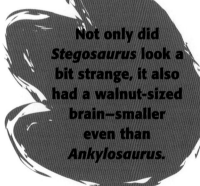

Not only did *Stegosaurus* look a bit strange, it also had a walnut-sized brain—smaller even than *Ankylosaurus*.

TRIASSIC	JURASSIC	CRETACEOUS

Cool dude

So, if the plates didn't protect the dinosaur, what did they do? Our best guess is that they helped regulate its temperature, rather like the crest of *Spinosaurus*. Another theory is that they were used in courtship displays.

Fact File

How to say it STE-goh-SORE-us
Meaning of name Roof lizard
Family Stegosauridae
Period Late Jurassic
Where found USA
Height 9 feet (2.8 meters)
Length 30 feet (9 meters)
Weight 3 tons (2,700 kilograms)
Food Plants
Special features Double row of plates

Defense

Just because the plates didn't offer much in the way of protection doesn't mean that *Stegosaurus* had no defense against attack. Its tail was armed with four fearsome spikes, and a dinosaur of this size could inflict a mighty thrashing on any foe.

CHASMOSAURUS

This spiky dinosaur had not only the three facial horns common to dinosaurs of this type, but also a series of smaller spikes running across the top of the frill at the back of its head: *Chasmosaurus* definitely sent a powerful message to predators to keep clear.

Frills and spills

The most striking feature of *Chasmosaurus* was its huge frill. It looked more impressive than it really was—in fact, it was little more than a frame with skin stretched over it. This made the frill quite weak and ineffective as a defense against attack. Paleontologists think it might have been used to impress females, or to make *Chasmosaurus* look more intimidating than it really was, or perhaps even to help regulate its body temperature.

Bone beds

Chasmosaurus remains have been discovered in so-called bone beds—areas where lots of bodies of the same species of dinosaur have been found. This evidence helps to support the theory that *Chasmosaurus* lived in large family groups.

TRIASSIC	JURASSIC	CRETACEOUS

Paleontologists believe the frill of a *Chasmosaurus* may have turned bright colors during the mating season.

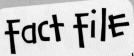

Fact File

How to say it kaz-moh-SORE-us
Meaning of name Chasm lizard
Family Ceratopidae
Period Late Cretaceous
Where found Canada, USA
Height 8 feet (2.4 meters)
Length 23 feet (7 meters)
Weight 1.4 tons (1,300 kilograms)
Food Plants
Special features Huge frill

PACHYCEPHALOSAURUS

Pachycephalosaurus had a very thick skull, yet it was nowhere near as tough as it looked.

Not such a tough guy

Originally, *Pachycephalosaurus* was thought to have used its thick skull to butt rivals with its head in courtship displays, like some sheep do. However, a close inspection of its head revealed none of the scar tissue that this action would cause. Some paleontologists also claim that although the dinosaur's skull was thick, it was not actually that hard and would break under this kind of impact.

Up and down

Pachycephalosaurus might have spent most of its time on two legs but, when grazing, it would happily drop down on all fours, just like a kangaroo. Since these dinosaurs were not very fast on two legs, they would also run off on all fours when they needed to make a quick getaway.

The nose of *Pachycephalosaurus* ended in a small beak. It probably tore off plants with its tiny teeth.

Fact File

How to say it PAK-ee-SEF-al-oh-SORE-us
Meaning of name Thick-headed lizard
Family Pachycephalosauridae
Period Late Cretaceous
Where found Canada, USA
Height 20 feet (6 meters)
Length 26 feet (8 meters)
Weight 2 tons (1,800 kilograms)
Food Plants
Special features Thick skull

KENTROSAURUS

This unusual-looking dinosaur was nowhere near as ferocious as it appeared. Part of the stegosaurid family, this particular species was found in eastern Africa.

Puzzling plates

Kentrosaurus had a striking combination of spikes and plates that ran down its back and tail. The upper part of the back had a double row of plates; the lower portion and tail a double row of spikes. The spikes appear to have been defensive but the plates are a little less easy to explain. Perhaps *Kentrosaurus* could make them change color as part of a courtship display. Or maybe they were for regulating the dinosaur's temperature; a series of blood vessels near the surface could help cool or heat the animal.

TRIASSIC JURASSIC CRETACEOUS

Small brain

Famously, the stegosaurids were a bit dim and *Kentrosaurus* was no exception. But although it couldn't help you do a crossword puzzle, its small brain was actually quite well developed for processing smells, so it had one good sense at least.

Fact File

How to say it KENT-row-SORE-us
Meaning of name Spiky lizard
Family Stegosauridae
Period Late Jurassic
Where found Tanzania
Height 6 feet 6 inches (2 meters)
Length 16 feet 5 inches (5 meters)
Weight 990 pounds (450 kilograms)
Food Plants
Special features Combination of body plates and spikes

The back legs of *Kentrosaurus* were longer than the front, which was a great advantage for this ground-feeding plant-eater.

PROTOCERATOPS

We know a lot about *Protoceratops* because paleontologists have been able to study them at every stage, from egg to adulthood.

Because it was small and slow-moving, *Protoceratops* lived in herds for protection.

Nesting

From the nesting sites that have been discovered, paleontologists know that *Protoceratops* were good parents. The mother would dig a hole in the ground before carefully laying the eggs so that they pointed outward. After the eggs hatched, the adults would stand guard to try to protect the young from predators.

Fact File

How to say it pro-toe-KAIR-a-tops
Meaning of name First horned face
Family Protoceratopidae
Period Late Cretaceous
Where found China, Mongolia
Height 2 feet 7 inches (0.8 meters)
Length 6 feet (1.8 meters)
Weight 880 pounds (400 kilograms)
Food Plants
Special features Early horned dinosaur

Threat

Protoceratops was one of the early horned dinosaurs, although actually its horn was little more than a bump on its nose. About the size of a sheep or a pig, and not a particularly fast mover, this dinosaur was prey to carnivores such as *Velociraptor*.

NODOSAURUS

This medium-sized, armored dinosaur was fairly placid if not disturbed, so it was quite safe—from a distance.

Same but different

Nodosaurus looked a bit like *Ankylosaurus*; they were both heavy, squat dinosaurs armed with bony plates. But *Nodosaurus* was slightly different—the tail had no leg-breaking club attachment and the armor lacked the spikes of *Ankylosaurus*. The mouth was different as well: it was much narrower than that of *Ankylosaurus*, which meant it couldn't eat every plant it came across. This armored heavyweight feasted upon only the softer and younger plants.

Nodosaurus was one of the first armored dinosaurs to be discovered in North America.

Fact File

How to say it no-doh-SORE-us
Meaning of name Node lizard
Family Nodosoridae
Period Early Cretaceous
Where found Namibia, South Africa, USA
Height 6 feet (1.8 meters)
Length 16 feet (5 meters)
Weight 3 tons (2,700 kilograms)
Food Plants
Special features Thick body armor

Defensive posture

Lacking any kind of weapon, *Nodosaurus* was limited in what action it could take during an attack by a predator. Not possessing the speed to run very far, it could only crouch close to the ground and wait until the meat-eater tired of trying to pierce its bony plates.

TRIASSIC   JURASSIC   CRETACEOUS

STEGOCERAS

Stegoceras was about the size of a large sheep and was the smallest member of the **Pachycephalosaurus** family. However, it shared all the same features—in particular, the controversial thick skull.

Growing pains

Like the other members of its family, *Stegoceras* were thought to butt each other with their heads in mating displays, but now this is thought not to be the case. Paleontologists have looked at the remains of *Stegoceras* skulls and discovered soft tissue. In the past, this was thought to absorb the impact of blows, but now we know that it is, in fact, a sign of bone growth—the remains being investigated were from young *Stegoceras*! Adult remains don't have this softer material.

Rooster booster

Examples of *Stegoceras* are few and far between, so paleontologists have not been able to answer the question of whether or not the adult male *Stegoceras* had a crest on its head like a cockerel. What do you think?

TRIASSIC	JURASSIC	CRETACEOUS

Fact File

How to say it STEG-o-ser-as
Meaning of name Horny roof
Family Pachycephalosauridae
Period Late Cretaceous
Where found Canada, USA
Height 16 feet 6 inches (5 meters)
Length 4 feet (1.2 meters)
Weight 172 pounds (78 kilograms)
Food Plants
Special features Thick skull

With its rounded eyes that faced forward, *Stegoceras* would have had good vision.

POLACANTHUS

Polacanthus is another example of a squat, armored dinosaur. It is from the early Cretaceous and was discovered in England.

Spiky personality

Like other armored dinosaurs, *Polacanthus* used its sizeable bulk and the bony plates on its upper body to defend itself from attack. Another distinctive line of protection was the array of spikes running down its back. These made it doubly difficult for a predator to get a grip and flip *Polacanthus* over in order to attack the softer underbelly.

Fact File

How to say it pol-a-KAN-thus
Meaning of name Many spines
Family Nodosauridae
Period Early Cretaceous
Where found England
Height 4 feet 7 inches (1.4 meters)
Length 16 feet 5 inches (5 meters)
Weight 1.1 tons (1,000 kilograms)
Food Plants
Special features Body armor and spikes

Embarrassing problem

Like *Ankylosaurus*, *Polacanthus* wasn't too fussy about what it ate—and it ate a lot. And, as you may imagine, this caused a problem, since its diet generated a lot of gas, which the dinosaur expelled freely, and often. This was definitely a dino to observe from upwind!

Although one of the first dinosaurs to be discovered, so far only three incomplete *Polacanthus* skeletons have been found.

STYRACOSAURUS

Despite its fearsome appearance, *Styracosaurus* was a peaceful dinosaur, like all members of the ceratopsid family. It lived in small herds and ate plants, migrating slowly across the continent in search of food.

Show-off

Those spiky horns on the edge of the head of *Styracosaurus* might look dangerous, but many paleontologists believe they were just for show. The pointy frill made the dinosaur appear bigger and more threatening than it really was.

Straight to the point

The frill may have been for show, but the horn of *Styracosaurus* was the real deal. At about 2 feet (0.6 meters) long, it made a formidable weapon. As if the horn wasn't enough of a threat, *Styracosaurus* had another important weapon in its armory—teamwork. When a predator approached, the herd closed together in a circle, with the young safely in the middle, while the adults presented a wall of horns to the oncoming foe.

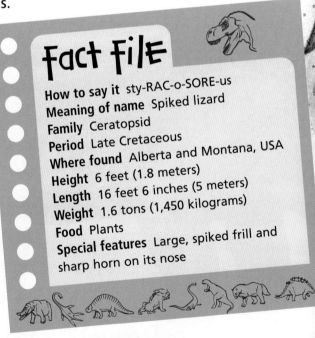

Fact File

How to say it sty-RAC-o-SORE-us
Meaning of name Spiked lizard
Family Ceratopsid
Period Late Cretaceous
Where found Alberta and Montana, USA
Height 6 feet (1.8 meters)
Length 16 feet 6 inches (5 meters)
Weight 1.6 tons (1,450 kilograms)
Food Plants
Special features Large, spiked frill and sharp horn on its nose

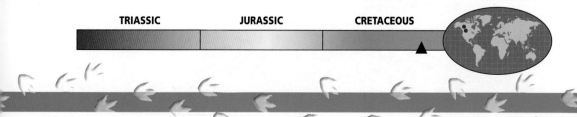

TRIASSIC   JURASSIC   CRETACEOUS

The frill of *Styracosaurus* may have been brightly colored to create a really impressive display.

WUERHOSAURUS

Wuerhosaurus was a Chinese member of the stegosaur family—one of the later examples—with lower, more rounded plates than its older relatives.

A bit slow

In common with other stegosaurids, *Wuerhosaurus* had one of the smallest brains in relation to its body size—the measure paleontologists use to judge dino intelligence. So they are likely to have been the least intelligent of all the dinosaurs. But just how bright do you have to be to eat leaves all day?

Thagomizer

Like *Stegosaurus*, its more famous cousin, *Wuerhosaurus* had a fearsome weapon at the end of its tail. These four sharp spikes were quite effective at warding off all but the biggest or most persistent of predators. The name that paleontologists have adopted for this

Wuerhosaurus is the last of the stegosaurs to be discovered to date. It may therefore be the last of its kind.

TRIASSIC   JURASSIC   CRETACEOUS

spiked club is "thagomizer," a term invented by the American illustrator Gary Larson in one of his cartoon strips. The tails of stegosaurid dinosaurs were probably more flexible than those of other dinosaurs, making them particularly suitable to use as weapons, lashing and whipping their enemies.

Fact File

How to say it WER-oh-SORE-us
Meaning of name Wuerho lizard
Family Stegosauridae
Period Early Cretaceous
Where found China
Height 6 feet 7 inches (2 meters)
Length 26 feet (8 meters)
Weight 4 tons (3,600 kilograms)
Food Plants
Special features Double row of plates and spiked tail

Picture credits

© Science Photo Library: front cover

© Shutterstock: back cover

© De Agostini Picture Library: title page; pages 4; 5; 6–9; 12–21; 24–25; 28–29

© Miles Kelly Publishing Ltd: pages 10–11

© Natural History Museum, London: pages 22–23

© Highlights for Children, Inc: pages 26–27

ARCTURUS

This edition published in 2014 by Arcturus Publishing Limited
26/27 Bickels Yard, 151–153 Bermondsey Street,
London SE1 3HA

Copyright © 2013 Arcturus Publishing Limited

ISBN: 978-1-84858-766-3
CH002613US
Supplier 15, Date 1113, Print run 2987

Printed in China